Colin Comma

is the busiest,

happiest,

and most cheerful

of the Puncs...

...and he

also loves

to sing.

morning,

In the mornings, from
7 o'clock until mid-day,
he is a postman.

In the afternoons, from
2 o'clock until 3 o'clock,
he is a window-cleaner,

and, in the evenings, from 7 o'clock until 9 o'clock, he delivers boxes of farm-fresh fruit, vegetables, and eggs.

He lives with his wife, Clarrie, and their two children, Chris and Chloe, at

Sweet Comma Cottage,
Punc Lane,
Commaton,

which is a large village near Commaford, not far from Commashott.

woof, woof,

When he was a small boy, his mother, who is called Cathy, noticed that he had a sweet, clear singing voice, which is not surprising, as his father, Caradoc,

Just after Colin had reached the age of six, Cathy decided that it was time he had singing lessons, so she took him to Mr Punctone, who is organist at the local church, and who could tell, after listening to a few high notes, that Colin's voice was very tuneful.

do, re, mi, fa, so, la...

howl, howl,

Not only did Colin become a star member
of the choir, singing songs from
the musicals, folk tunes,
country, hillbilly,
ballads, etc.,

he also taught himself
to play the guitar,
and, later, joined a pop group
called the Rolling Puncs.

particularly enjoys picking out the kind of parcels **,** packages **,** letters **,** etc. **,** that make people happy **,** but he hates junk mail.

"What a waste of paper, and wood, and trees,"

he grumbles, as he sorts out leaflets, pamphlets, hand-outs, circulars, samples, and so on.

Colin loves being out of doors, as well as chatting to people, which is why he chose to be a postman.

However, when he is on his rounds, pushing his trolley, he often bursts into song.

(Generally, no-one can hear him because of the traffic!)

After lunch every day, Colin goes on his window-cleaning rounds. He loads up the van with his extending ladder,

his rubber bucket,

his shammy leather,

and his squeegee,

and sets off round the village.

Of course, he sings as he works, and, believe it or not, his favourite song is

'When I'm cleaning windows'.

As might be expected, Colin's customers are the same people as on his mail rounds.

They are, for example, at Numbers 3, 7, 14 and 24, Comma Close,...

...and Numbers 11**,** 19 and 22**,** Punc Crescent.

He also has a customer at
Number 20**,** Punc
Lane**,** who is called
Cherry Comma**,**
and who happens to
be his cousin.

Colin always has to be on the move, morning, noon, and night.

When he has finished cleaning windows, he jumps into his van, drives to the farm shop down the lane, and starts work again, picking up boxes of fruit, vegetables, and eggs, and loading them into his van.

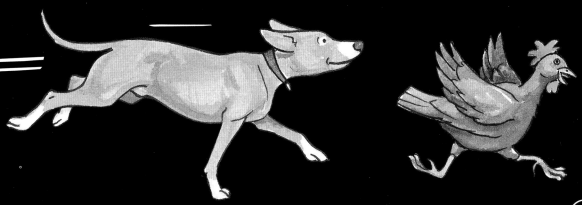

Sometimes, on summer evenings,
but not in the dark, Colin's children,
Chloe, aged nine, and Chris, aged
eleven, are allowed to help him deliver
the boxes, which they wheel to the
customers' doors in an old pram.

23

During the holidays, Colin, Clarrie, Chloe and Chris spend a lot of their time going for long walks. Because they are true country folk, they are very careful about keeping to

the paths,

following the signposts,

shutting gates,

putting litter in bins,

and generally looking after

the countryside.

Now and again, the whole family pack
their bags into the van, and visit
their Irish cousins, the O'Commas
of County Kilpunc.

Occasionally, Colin and two of his
cousins, Liam and Callum, go to the
local club for an evening out. Colin takes
his guitar, Liam his banjo, and Callum
his fiddle, and, with the other
customers, they have a happy time
singing their favourite Irish songs.

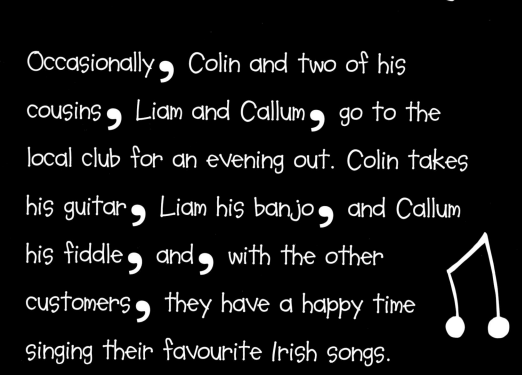

Colin gets on well with the other Puncs, except Fergus Full Stop.

While Fergus is trying to do his job, bringing
everything to a quick Full Stop, Colin is always
getting in the way, wheeling his trolley,
propping up his ladder,

parking his van,

wandering along

the lanes,

endlessly on the

move, never

knowing when

to stop.

As you should know by now,

Colin, as well as being cheerful, kind, helpful, energetic, and always singing, is so busy that he never knows when to stop, and although he is very useful for breaking up sentences, like this one, he is quite unable to bring them to an end, so, Fergus Full Stop has to come to the rescue, like this.

Colin's Checklist

- **To avoid getting into a muddle, use commas to separate items in a list, like this:**
Colin sorts out leaflets, pamphlets, hand-outs, circulars, samples, etc.

- **A comma can separate two or more adjectives (describing words), like this:**
Colin is the busiest, happiest, and most cheerful of the Puncs.

- **Use a comma to write dates:**
Wednesday, 21 January, 2003.

- **Commas are useful for breaking up instructions, like this one:**
Turn left, take the second traffic lights, go past the school, and then straight on to Colin Comma's cottage.

- **Use a comma to join two halves of a sentence, like this:**
Although Colin only delivers fish once a week, his van always smells fishy.

- **Use a pair of commas to separate a fact or explanation from the rest of the sentence, like this:**
In the mornings, between 7 o'clock and mid-day, Colin is a postman.

- **Introductory words like 'well', 'now', 'yes', 'however', 'after', 'although', 'as', 'since', 'when', are followed by a comma:**
However, no-one can hear Colin sing because of the noise of the traffic.

- **Use a comma to join 2 phrases when a link word like 'and', 'but', 'for' or 'so' is used:**
Colin likes to be busy, but sometimes he runs away with himself.

- **A comma can separate a fact from a question, like this:**
Colin Comma is a busy Punc, isn't he?

- **Use a comma to introduce or interrupt quotations, like this:**
Colin said, "I'm busy".
"I'm busy," said Colin, "I'll do it later".

- **Use a comma to help make something clear, like this:**
To Colin, commas make perfect sense.

- **Use a comma to show thousands:**
1,000   2,000   3,000

- **Remember:** Commas and apostrophes look the same but appear in different places within a sentence.